D0793636

NATIVE NATIONS OF THE
SOUTHWEST

BY BARBARA KRASNER

Published by The Child's World®
1980 Lookout Drive • Mankato, MN 56003-1705
800-599-READ • www.childsworld.com
Acknowledgments
The Child's World®: Mary Berendes, Publishing Director
Red Line Editorial: Editorial direction and production
The Design Lab: Design
Content Consultant: Donald D. Pepion, Ed.D.,
College Professor, Anthropology: Native American Studies
New Mexico State University

Photographs ©: Ross D. Franklin/AP Images, cover, 2;
Brooklyn Museum, 1, 36; Michael Quinn/National Park
Service, 3 (top), 7; Felicia Fonseca/AP Images, 3 (middle top),
16; Kobby Dagan/Shutterstock Images, 3 (middle bottom),
3 (bottom), 23, 35; Tom Willard/Shutterstock Images, 5,
39; Amy Sussman/Smithsonian's National Museum of the
American Indian/AP Images, 9; Catherine Karnow/Corbis,
10; Anders Ryman/Corbis, 12; Pauline Arrillaga/AP Images,
14; Public Domain, 15; Wolfgang Staudt CC 2.0, 18; Library of
Congress, 19; Susan Montoya Bryan/AP Images, 20, 29; Erin
Whittaker/National Park Service, 21; iStockphoto, 22; Debby
Wong/Corbis, 25; Jeff Geissler/AP Images, 26; Natalia
Bratslavsky/Shutterstock Images, 27; Ryan Brennecke/The
Sun/AP Images, 30; Stringer/USA/Reuters/Newscom, 32;
Terry W Ryder/Shutterstock Images, 33

ISBN: 9781634070362
LCCN: 2014959807
Printed in the United States of America
Mankato, MN
July, 2015
PAO2269

33614080655557

ABOUT THE AUTHOR

Freelance author Barbara Krasner writes nonfiction, fiction, and poetry for children and adults. She holds an MFA in Writing for Children & Young Adults from the Vermont College of Fine Arts and teaches children's literature and creative writing at William Paterson University in New Jersey, where she is currently pursuing a master's in public history.

Nedallas Hammill of the Navajo, Apache, Pima, and other Native Nations performs a hoop dance at a competition in Phoenix, Arizona.

TABLE OF CONTENTS

Gulf of
Alaska

Hudson
Bay

CANADA

PACIFIC

OCEAN

ATLANTIC

OCEAN

UNITED STATES

KEY

SOUTHWEST
NATIVE NATIONS

N
W   E
S

MEXICO

Gulf of
Mexico

4

CHAPTER ONE

SOUTHWEST NATIVE NATIONS

The American Southwest is a land of spectacular canyons and breathtaking mountains. Its deserts hold ancient rock formations and unique plants. The region includes Arizona and New Mexico and parts of Utah, Colorado, Oklahoma, and

Built in the 1100s AD, no one lives in Wupatki Pueblo in Arizona today. But it remains part of the cultural and spiritual heritage of the region's Native People.

Texas. Many generations of Native Nations have called the Southwest home. Their oral histories tell of the spirits and gods that live in the canyons, mountains, and **mesas**.

Some Native Nations of the Southwest include the Apache, Hopi, Navajo, Pima, Pueblo, Quechan, Tohono O'odham, and the largest Pueblo Nation, Zuni. They live on **reservations** and settlements in Arizona, New Mexico, and parts of Utah and Oklahoma. Some once lived in Colorado and other surrounding states.

The Native Nations of the Southwest had different ways of life. But their cultures have some similarities because they all had to adapt to the dry region. They were challenged by the lack of water, but they all farmed. They also hunted and gathered to provide for themselves. They traveled across large areas of land to find what they needed to survive.

The first Europeans, the Spanish, came to the area in the 1500s. They claimed the entire region as the colony of Mexico. Later Mexico became independent and governed much of the Southwest. The United States took control of the region in 1848 after the Mexican-American War.

The Apache, Navajo, and others fought to keep their land. But by the mid-1800s, many Southwest Native Nations signed treaties with the U.S. government. The treaties would protect their people from attacks and allow them to keep their hunting and fishing rights. The treaties would also give them federal recognition. Recognition as a Native Nation meant the U.S. government promised the people health and education

Dance is a feature of many Nation's celebrations and ceremonies. Arizona's Dishchii' Bikoh' Apache Group dances the Apache Crown Dance at a Native American Heritage Month celebration at the Grand Canyon.

services and some financial benefits. The government recognized their **sovereignty**, the right to govern themselves. In exchange, the government took much of the Native lands away. The Southwest Nations were forced to live on reservations.

Despite the treaties, state and federal governments broke promises. Promised goods, money, or services did not come. New laws changed the treaties without Native consent. Struggles for land and water rights continue today. Native Peoples in Arizona and New Mexico did not have the right to vote as U.S. citizens until 1948. They had to win lawsuits to get that right.

Children were removed from their families and sent to boarding schools, sometimes far away from home. Young people were cut off from their traditions and language. Some traditions were lost. Languages became endangered. Today, these Southwest Nations hold onto their traditions and pass them down from generation to generation. They share **oral histories** telling the origins of their people. They celebrate their religions with traditional ceremonies. Some nations avoid photography of these events for religious reasons. They believe these religious

In November 2014, the National Museum of the American Indian celebrated its twentieth anniversary. The museum's New York City location opened its Glittering World exhibit. It has more than 300 pieces of jewelry made by the Yazzie family, who are Navajo artists. They craft jewelry from silver, turquoise, and coral.

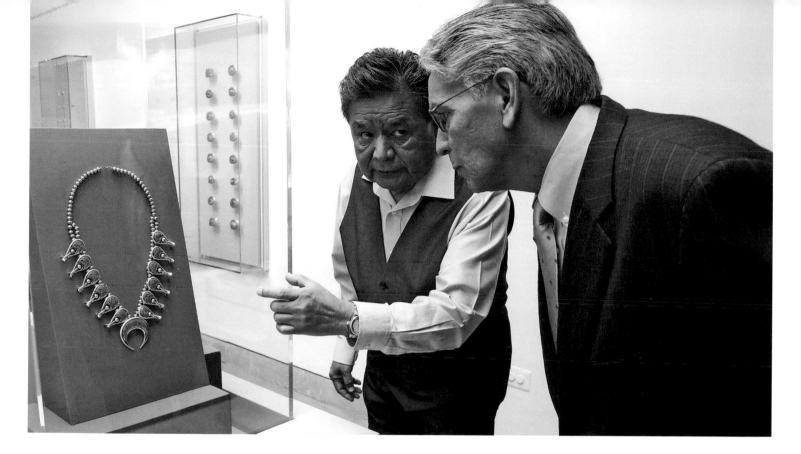

Lee Yazzie, left, points out a squash blossom necklace at his museum exhibition at the National Museum of the American Indian.

traditions should be private and for Native followers only.

Most of the Nations elect a council that governs them. But among the Pueblo, each community governs itself. **Gaming** and casinos help members of some nations earn a living. Others make money from crafts and tourism. Some make a living from natural resources, such as metals, oil, and gas. Unemployment and poverty challenge the Native Nations. The nations work hard to help their communities survive.

CHAPTER TWO

APACHE

The White Mountain Apache Tribe Fair and Rodeo celebrates the Apache heritage of horseback riding.

The Apache are historically known as fierce fighters. Apache defense against Europeans and then the United States lasted for centuries. The conflict produced strong resisters, including Geronimo. Geronimo (1829–1909), took a stand against whites when his people were restricted to the San Carlos Reservation in Arizona. Today the Apache Nation is made up of eight federally recognized groups.

The San Carlos Apache Tribe Reservation in Arizona covers nearly 2 million acres (0.8 million ha). Fishers catch trout, bass, catfish, and other fish in its four lakes and two rivers. The nation has more than 15,000 people. However, unemployment on the reservation is high compared to the rest of Arizona.

The Fort Apache Reservation in Arizona is home to the White Mountain Apache Tribe. It has more than 13,000 members. The reservation includes Mount Baldy, which is sacred to the nation. The Jicarilla Apache Nation Reservation is in New Mexico with approximately 3,600 members. They are active in protecting their pine forests and mountain landscapes.

The Mescalero Apache Tribe of New Mexico has close to 4,000 members. Its 463,000-acre (187,000 ha) reservation includes the heart of the nation's traditional territory. One of the nation's most important ceremonies is its puberty rite of passage. The four-day ceremony for girls includes dancing, feasts, and ancient blessings and rituals.

The Fort Sill Reservation in Oklahoma has an enrollment of 700 people. Members have been working through the courts to move

SAY IT			
	one	dalaa	(DA-lah)
	two	naakii	(NΔ-kee)
	three	kái'ii	(KΔ-ee-ee)

At the San Carlos Apache Tribe Reservation, a girl celebrates her puberty rite of passage. She is painted white with clay and cornmeal.

the reservation back to traditional lands in New Mexico. The group intends to open the Apache Homelands Casino there, which will give jobs to almost 1,000 people.

Smaller nations include the Yavapai Apache, who live on the Fort McDowell reservation in Arizona. They run a casino. The Tonto Apache Nation has approximately 110 enrolled members. Native artists there are known for their baskets and beadwork.

Adam Hines, an 11-year-old Yavapai Apache, won the North American title at the International Kickboxing Federation tournament held in the summer of 2014. Adam lives in Arizona. His coach hopes he will inspire other kids to work out with him. Obesity is a big problem in the Native community, as it is throughout the United States. Working out in the gym like Adam can help kids be healthy.

CHAPTER THREE

HOPI

Hopi cultural preservation experts work with Navajo colleagues to preserve ancient sites.

The Hopi Nation lives in 12 villages across three mesas in northeastern Arizona. These mesas are known as First Mesa, Second Mesa, and Third Mesa. Each village governs itself. Although many Hopi live in these **adobe** villages, many leave

Some Oraibi structures are ancient.

their communities to find work. Together, approximately 10,000 people are members of the nation. The Navajo surround the Hopi. The two nations disagreed about their borders for many years but finally reached an agreement in 2009.

The Hopi village of Oraibi is one of the oldest settlements in the United States where people have lived continuously. It dates back to 1150. Originally, the village stood at the foot of the Third Mesa. Later it moved to the top of the mesa.

The Hopi believe they have a mission to take care of their land. They strive to

SAY IT			
	dog	Pòoko	(POE-koh)
	horse	Kawayo	(kah-WHY-oh)
	bear	Hoonaw	(HOE-now)

The Hopi High School cross-country team continues the Hopi tradition of distance running.

respect the land and its resources as farmers. Centuries ago they mined the coal in the area. They stopped when the Spaniards arrived. In the 1960s, the Hopi and Navajo allowed the Peabody Western Coal Company to mine the coal. However, over the decades, the mine caused much pollution. Mining has harmed their water. Miners suffered long-term health problems such as black lung disease. The nation used their land and water rights to halt the mining on Hopi land in 2006.

Unlike some Native Nations of the Southwest, the Hopi do not run any casinos. Gambling goes against their nation's values. But they do run two hotels. They also have a cultural center. Many members practice Hopi traditions and speak their language. They ask visitors to respect their privacy during religious ceremonies. They hold seasonal dances and rituals that honor nature and celebrate their role in taking care of Earth.

The Hopi have produced some great runners. Louis Tewanima (1888–1969) was a member of the 1908 and 1912 U.S. Olympic track teams. He won a silver medal in 1912. In November 2014, Hopi High School took first place in the Arizona boys' cross-country championship. It marked the 25th straight win for the school and set a national record.

CHAPTER FOUR

NAVAJO

The hogan is a traditional Navajo style of home.

The Navajo Nation, Navajoland, is the largest Native Nation in the United States. It has more area than Vermont, New Hampshire, Rhode Island, Connecticut, and Delaware combined. The land stretches across four reservations in Arizona,

New Mexico, and Utah. There are 273,000 members of the Navajo Nation.

In 1864, the U.S. government forced thousands of Navajo to walk several hundred miles from their homes in Arizona to a reservation in New Mexico. This was called the Long Walk. Soldiers on horseback forced everyone to walk many miles each day. Hundreds died during the forced march.

A treaty in 1868 gave the Navajo back some of their land. For many years, the Navajo argued over land claims with the Hopi.

The Navajo lived in houses made of wood and mud. Called **hogans**, these houses usually have six or eight sides. Doors open to the east to welcome the rising run. Many Navajo still have hogans, though most new

A Navajo woman weaves a blanket, ca. 1920-1930.

A Navajo economic development officer points out a future solar panel installation, which will provide power and jobs to the reservation.

buildings are for ceremonies, not for people to live in.

The Navajo people are known for their art, especially their work with silver and turquoise. Turquoise is important to Navajo religious practices. It represents a person's well-being. Basket and rug weaving, pottery, and sand painting are also traditional arts.

Sand paintings tell stories of Navajo gods, dances, and rituals.

Unemployment runs high among the Navajo, as it does for many Native Nations. The Navajo initially rejected gaming, but recently chose to open casinos. The first casino opened in New Mexico in 2008.

During World War II (1939–1945), the U.S. military brought together a group of Navajos to create a secret code. The code talkers would send and receive brief radio messages in Pacific battles that the enemy would not be able to understand. The Navajo language was ideal for code. The language hadn't been written down. Plus, a word could take on different meanings depending on how it was said. They made up words like "iron fish," which meant "submarine." The Navajo code was never broken. Keeping messages secret saved lives in battle and helped win the war.

Navajo code talker Dan Akee served with the U.S. Marine Corps in the Pacific during World War II.

hello	Yá'át'ééh	(ya-aht-AY)	
good morning	Yá'át'ééh abini	(ya-aht-AY ab-IN-eh)	SAY IT
goodbye	Hágoónee'	(ha-GAW-aw-neh)	

CHAPTER FIVE

PIMA

The Pima call themselves Akimel O'odham, or "People of the River." The Spanish gave them the name Pima. The exact meaning of that name is not known. Ancient Pima ancestors built complex irrigation systems around the Gila River. These People of the River used irrigation to farm.

The Pima consider the ancient Hohokam people their ancestors and protect their cultural legacy.

Pima women show traditional dress and basket styles during a parade.

Farming became difficult, though, when dams and nonnative farmers brought changes. From 1880 to 1920, the nation suffered famine and starvation. The U.S. government provided much-needed food. But the change in diet led to health problems the Pima still face today. The Coolidge Dam on the Gila River helped to restore water to the reservation. Farming once again was possible, and the starvation ended.

The Pima live on two Arizona reservations. Gila River was established by treaty in 1859. It has more than 20,000 members. Farming remains a major business. The Pima grow alfalfa, barley, citrus fruits, cotton, grapes, lettuce, melons, and onions. They host boat races on local lakes and car races at Wild Horse Pass Motorsports Park. They also run the Gila River Casinos and several golf courses.

The Salt River Reservation was established in 1879 near Phoenix. Its Native enrollment is about 9,000 people. It runs a casino and resort. But it is known for the Pavilions, the largest retail complex on Native lands in the United States.

Ira Hayes, a member of the Pima Nation, was one of the U.S. marines who helped raise the flag at Iwo Jima during World War II. He became a national hero when the photograph of that moment was sent worldwide.

Baseball is big business for the Pima. They own Salt River Fields at Talking Stick, the spring training ground for two major league baseball teams. The Colorado Rockies share the facility with the Arizona Diamondbacks. Salt River Fields is also the home stadium of the Salt River Rafters, a minor league team in the Arizona Fall League.

The Salt River Reservation operates the Salt River Fields baseball stadium.

CHAPTER SIX

PUEBLO

Santo Domingo Pueblo artist Robert Tenorio mixes traditional styles with modern imagery in his work.

The Spanish were the first Europeans to meet the Native Nations of the Southwest. Over generations, Spanish culture has influenced Native ways of life. Some Nations today have kept the names the Spanish used for them, such as Pueblo, Santo

Buildings at Taos Pueblo in New Mexico have been lived in for more than 1,000 years.

Domingo, and Santa Clara. Spanish religious customs have also influenced Native Nations, including the Pueblo.

The Pueblo people live in 19 **pueblos** in New Mexico, plus one in Arizona and one in Texas. Some include the Acoma, Isleta,

Laguna (the largest), Taos, and Zuni. Among them, they speak five languages. They once lived on land that stretched across New Mexico, Arizona, and Colorado. More than 62,000 people call themselves members of the Pueblo.

Some of the nations, such as the Pueblo of Isleta, combine modern business with traditional ways. They run a successful casino, resort, and golf course. They also offer fishing and camping trips for tourists all year long. Many Isleta members farm. As some other Pueblos do, they follow the Catholic faith. In the late 1500s, the Spaniards gave each pueblo or nation a patron saint. Saint Augustine is the patron saint of the Isleta. Some traditional songs, dances, and rituals continue to be performed. The Isleta have nearly 4,000 members.

The Pueblo of Laguna is one of the largest Nations, with more than 8,000 members. Their ceremonies are meant to bring rain and control the weather for farming. Some Pueblo ceremonies take place in chambers called *kivas*. The walls are often painted with geometric patterns, scenes from daily life, or religious images.

Patricia Michaels, a textile and fashion designer, brought her Taos Pueblo heritage to television. She appeared on Lifetime TV's Project Runway in 2013. She won the runner-up title. She was the first Native designer to compete on the program. She was also the first Native to show her designs at New York City's most famous fashion show, Mercedes-Benz Fashion Week at Lincoln Center. Since Michaels's appearance, two other Natives, one from the Northwest and one from Hawaii, have been contestants on the show.

Joshua Madalena, a leader of the Jemez Pueblo, speaks in court. He was defending the Jemez Pueblo claim to land in New Mexico. They consider this land a spiritually important part of their homeland.

The Pueblo of Acoma is home to Sky City. It is a pueblo on a mesa 367 feet (112 m) high. The pueblo dates back nearly 1,000 years. The Acoma have nearly 5,000 members. Among other businesses, they run a casino and cultural center. The large cultural center includes a museum with exhibits on Acoma culture, art, and history.

CHAPTER SEVEN

QUECHAN

The Quechan Nation runs a program that teaches its language.

The Quechan (KWUH-tsan) used to be known as the Yuma or Yuman people. For hundreds of years, they fought the Apache and other nations. They sought control of the Colorado River flood plains. These plains provided fertile farmland. The

Quechan also controlled the best crossing point of the river until the U.S. Army defeated them in the 1850s.

The Fort Yuma Quechan Reservation was established by treaty in 1884 in Arizona. The Colorado River forms the border between Arizona and California. The reservation is on both sides of the river and is therefore in both Arizona and California. It also borders Mexico. The Arizona city and county are called Yuma after the former name of the nation. The Quechan Nation has approximately 2,500 people.

The nation has a sand and gravel business and leases its farmland to nonnative farmers. Tourism, especially during the winter months, helps members earn a living. They run a bingo hall, casino, resort, and several recreational vehicle (RV) parks. The Quechan Cultural Center in the casino shares Native artifacts and history.

Quechan beadwork is a women-only art form. Historically, Quechan women and others of the Southwest wore beaded collars or capes with geometric patterns. Women today make the collars to wear for celebrations and ceremonies and to sell.

Each March the Quechan hold a two-day **powwow**. The event celebrates Quechan heritage with dancing and singing. Nearly 20 different dances are performed. At the event, people can buy Quechan jewelry, baskets, pottery, and foods such as fry bread. The San Pasqual Unified School District of California, just two miles north of the Quechan reservation in Arizona, hosts the event. Students learn about and share their heritage and get to volunteer in their community.

CHAPTER EIGHT

TOHONO O'ODHAM

A simple fence marks the U.S.-Mexican border at places on the Tohono O'odham Reservation.

The Tohono O'odham, or "Desert People," used to be called the Papago. They are the second-largest nation in Arizona, after the Navajo. The Tohono O'odham are closely related to the Pima, or Akimel O'odham, the River People.

San Xavier Mission in Tucson, Arizona, is on a Tohono O'odham reservation.

Traditionally, the Tohono O'odham hunted and gathered. They traded with other nations for what they needed. A Jesuit missionary visited them in the 1600s. The Jesuits converted the Tohono O'odham to the Catholic faith, which many follow today.

When Mexico sold land to the United States, Tohono O'odham land was split between Arizona and Mexico. Some Tohono O'odham communities still live in Mexico. Membership in the nation allows community members to cross the U.S.-Mexico border freely. However, increased trouble with security and immigration has caused issues. Nation members report being harassed by the border guards during their legal crossings. The nation also has to deal with smuggling and illegal border crossings on its lands.

The Tohono O'odham have approximately 28,000 members. Half of them live on several reservations. The first reservation, San Xavier, was established in 1874. Here the nation runs three casinos and a mining business. The second reservation, Gila Bend, was created in 1882. The third and largest is Tohono O'odham, formed in 1917. Florence Village, a 20-acre (8 ha) piece of land, was added in 1978. Some members harvest a desert fruit called **saguaro** from a cactus and make jams, jellies, and wine with it.

The Tohono O'odham run a community college, a cultural center, and a museum. They also host a rodeo each February. Still, the nation has one of the lowest per-person incomes of all Native Nations in the United States. The nation began construction on the West Valley Resort & Casino in 2014. The business should bring approximately 3,000 jobs to the area.

CHAPTER NINE

ZUNI

The Zuni are a Pueblo people. They were the first Native Nation the Spaniards met when they arrived in the Southwest in 1539. Spain claimed the Zuni land and the southwest region until 1821, when Mexico won its independence. In 1848, the land transferred to the United States. Once the owners of millions of acres of land

Zuni women participate in a parade, displaying traditional clothing and pottery styles.

863-0300

Kachina doll, late 19th century, made from wood, wool, horsehair, and feathers

throughout the Southwest, the Zuni have been fighting for their land and water rights in the courts of several states. They lost much of their land due to western nonnative settlement, U.S. government claims, and the building of a railroad. Their reservation is 450,000 acres (180,000 ha), in addition to other land holdings in New Mexico and Arizona.

The Zuni are the largest of the Pueblo Nations, with more than 10,000 members. They have their own language and culture, partly because they are isolated from other Pueblos. The language is taught in the schools and most Zunis speak it.

Members make their living mostly from the arts and from Zuni businesses. But tourism is also a big moneymaker. The nation runs a museum and heritage center. Visitors to the reservation can take a walking tour of a historic pueblo. They can also visit the site where the Zuni first met the Spaniards. Zuni members and visitors alike enjoy catching trout, bass, and other fish on Zuni land.

Zuni celebrate many events during the year. Some are religious and involve masked men, called **kachinas**. These kachinas represent spirits. The nation holds a ceremonial dance to greet winter. In the dance, they bid farewell to the old year

and ask for blessings for the new year. The Zuni keep many ceremonies private from outsiders.

SAY IT			
	welcome	Keshshi	(kehsh-SHEE)
	mother	Tsitda	(TSEEP-da)
	father	Datchu	(DAP-chu)

The arts are important to many Zuni, and they are known worldwide for their skill. Artists work with silver, turquoise, and other natural materials to make jewelry, pottery, beadwork, carved stone animals, and kachina dolls. Much of the work is actually done in the home. Up to 80 percent of Zuni households are involved in creating art. The activity helps hold the community together and continue their traditions.

GLOSSARY

adobe (uh-DOH-bee) Adobe is sun-dried brick made of clay and straw. Adobe pueblos are traditional homes to many Native Nations of the Southwest.

gaming (GEY-ming) Gaming is another word for gambling. Many Native Nations support their local communities through gaming businesses.

hogans (hoh-GAWNZ) Hogans are traditional Navajo dwellings made of wood and earth and covered with mud. Many Navajo today still have hogans on their land.

kachinas (kuh-CHEE-nuhz) Kachinas are ancestral spirits represented by masked dancers or dolls. The Hopi and Pueblo Nations hold celebration dances where members wear masks as kachinas.

mesas (MEH-suhz) Mesas are land formations with flat tops and steep walls. Mesas are unique to the southwestern United States.

oral histories (AWR-uhl HIS-tuh-rees) Oral histories are the history and memories of a people told out loud. Some oral histories tell how Native Peoples came to live on their lands.

powwow (POU-wou) A powwow is a social gathering of Native Americans that usually includes dancing. Many Native Nations have a yearly powwow to celebrate their culture and traditions.

pueblos (PWEB-lohs) Pueblos are places made of adobe or stone where many families live. Many Southwest Native Peoples live in pueblos.

reservations (rez-er-VAY-shuhns) Reservations are areas of land set aside for Native American use. Reservations are run by their own governments and provide services to their residents.

saguaro (suh-GWAHR-oh) A saguaro is a kind of desert cactus that bears edible fruit. The Tohono O'odham use saguaro to make jellies and jams.

sovereignty (SOV-rin-tee) Sovereignty is the independent power to govern. Native sovereignty grants Native Nations the right to govern themselves.

TO LEARN MORE

BOOKS

Croy, Anita. *Ancient Pueblo: Archaeology Unlocks the Secrets of America's Past.* Washington, D.C.: National Geographic, 2007.

McDaniel, Melissa. *Southwest Indians.* Chicago: Heinemann, 2012.

Roberts, Russell. *The Apache of the Southwest.* Kennett Square, PA: Purple Toad Publishing, 2014.

WEB SITES

Visit our Web site for links about Native Nations of the Southwest:
childsworld.com/links

Note to Parents, Teachers, and Librarians: We routinely verify our Web links to make sure they are safe and active sites. So encourage your readers to check them out!